NIRVANA

ISBN 978-1-4950-3057-4

7777 W. BLUEMOUND RD. P.O. BOX 13819 MILWAUKEE, WI 53213

In Australia Contact:
Hal Leonard Australia Pty. Ltd.
4 Lentara Court
Cheltenham, Victoria, 3192 Australia
Email: ausadmin@halleonard.com.au

Visit Hal Leonard Online at
www.halleonard.com

ABOUT A GIRL

Words and Music by
KURT COBAIN

ALL APOLOGIES

Words and Music by
KURT COBAIN

Jazz Waltz (♩ = 184)

With pedal

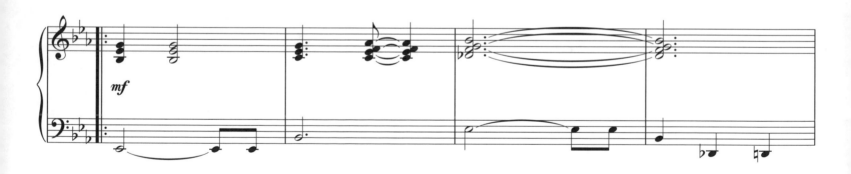

COME AS YOU ARE

Words and Music by
KURT COBAIN

DUMB

Words and Music by
KURT COBAIN

Easy Bounce (♩ = 126)

mp

Pedal as needed

sim.

mf

HEART SHAPED BOX

Words and Music by
KURT COBAIN

LITHIUM

Words and Music by
KURT COBAIN

Jazz/Funk Fusion (♩ = 132)

With pedal

IN BLOOM

Words and Music by
KURT COBAIN

Bright Swing ($\quad$ = 180)

34

To Coda ⊕

THE MAN WHO SOLD THE WORLD

Words and Music by
DAVID BOWIE

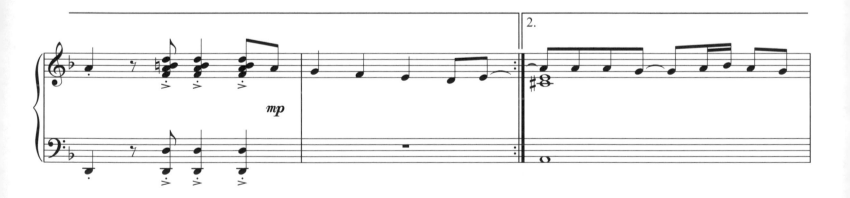

(NEW WAVE) POLLY

Words and Music by
KURT COBAIN

Bluesy Shuffle (♩ = 120)

To Coda

D.S. al Coda

ON A PLAIN

Words and Music by
KURT COBAIN

SMELLS LIKE TEEN SPIRIT

Words and Music by KURT COBAIN,
KRIST NOVOSELIC and DAVE GROHL

Cool Swing ($\quad$ = 132)

Pedal sparingly

RAPE ME

Words and Music by
KURT COBAIN

Slow Shuffle (♩ = 104)

p

With pedal

mp

cresc.

ALL JAZZED UP!

FROM HAL LEONARD

In this series, pop hits receive unexpected fresh treatments. Uniquely reimagined and crafted for intermediate piano solo, these favorites have been All Jazzed Up!

COLDPLAY

Clocks • Don't Panic • Every Teardrop Is a Waterfall • Fix You • Magic • Paradise • The Scientist • A Sky Full of Stars • Speed of Sound • Trouble • Viva La Vida • Yellow.
00149026 Intermediate Piano Solo.............. $12.99

DISNEY

Belle • Circle of Life • Cruella De Vil • Ev'rybody Wants to Be a Cat • It's a Small World • Let It Go • Mickey Mouse March • Once upon a Dream • Part of Your World • Supercalifragilisticexpialidocious • Under the Sea • When She Loved Me.
00151072 Intermediate Piano Solo.............. $12.99

J.S. BACH

Air on the G String • Aria • Bist du bei mir (Be Thou with Me) • Gavotte • Jesu, Joy of Man's Desiring • Largo • March • Minuet in G • Musette • Sheep May Safely Graze • Siciliano • Sleepers, Awake (Wachet Auf).
00151064 Intermediate Piano Solo.............. $12.99

NIRVANA

About a Girl • All Apologies • Come as You Are • Dumb • Heart Shaped Box • In Bloom • Lithium • The Man Who Sold the World • On a Plain • (New Wave) Polly • Rape Me • Smells like Teen Spirit.
00149025 Intermediate Piano Solo.............. $12.99

STEVIE WONDER

As • Ebony and Ivory • For Once in My Life • I Just Called to Say I Love You • I Wish • Isn't She Lovely • My Cherie Amour • Ribbon in the Sky • Signed, Sealed, Delivered I'm Yours • Sir Duke • Superstition • You Are the Sunshine of My Life.
00149090 Intermediate Piano Solo.............. $12.99

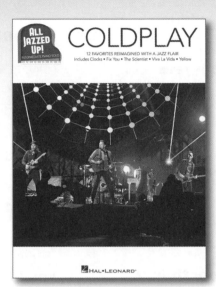

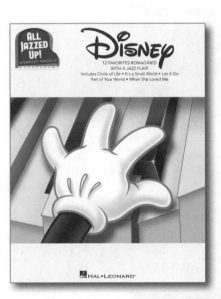

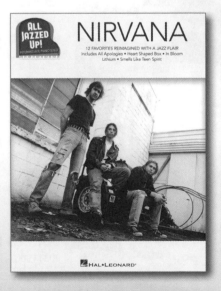

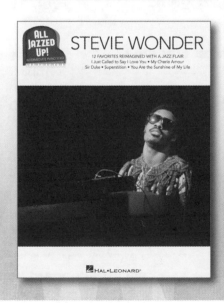

Prices, contents and availability subject to change without notice.

Disney characters and artwork
© Disney Enterprises, Inc.

HAL•LEONARD® CORPORATION
7777 W. BLUEMOUND RD. P.O. BOX 13819 MILWAUKEE, WI 53213

www.halleonard.com

1015

jazz piano solos series

vol. 1 miles davis
00306521............................$15.99

vol. 2 jazz blues
00306522............................$15.99

vol. 3 latin jazz
00310621............................$15.99

vol. 4 bebop jazz
00310709............................$15.99

vol. 5 cool jazz
00310710............................$15.99

vol. 6 hard bop
00310711............................$15.99

vol. 7 smooth jazz
00310727............................$15.99

vol. 8 jazz pop
00311786............................$15.99

vol. 9 duke ellington
00311787............................$15.99

vol. 10 jazz ballads
00311788............................$15.99

vol. 11 soul jazz
00311789............................$15.99

vol. 12 swinging jazz
00311797............................$15.99

vol. 13 jazz gems
00311899............................$15.99

vol. 14 jazz classics
00311900............................$15.99

vol. 15 bossa nova
00311906............................$15.99

vol. 16 disney
00312121............................$16.99

vol. 17 antonio carlos jobim
00312122............................$15.99

vol. 18 modern jazz quartet
00307270............................$16.99

vol. 19 bill evans
00307273............................$16.99

vol. 20 gypsy jazz
00307289............................$16.99

vol. 21 new orleans jazz piano solos
00312169............................$16.99

vol. 22 classic jazz
00001529............................$16.99

vol. 23 jazz for lovers
00312548............................$16.99

vol. 24 john coltrane
00307395............................$16.99

vol. 25 christmas songs
00101790............................$16.99

vol. 26 george gershwin
00103353............................$16.99

vol. 27 late night jazz
00312547............................$16.99

vol. 30 cole porter
00123364............................$16.99

vol. 31 cocktail piano
00123366............................$16.99

vol. 32 johnny mercer
00123367............................$16.99

vol. 33 gospel
00127079............................$16.99

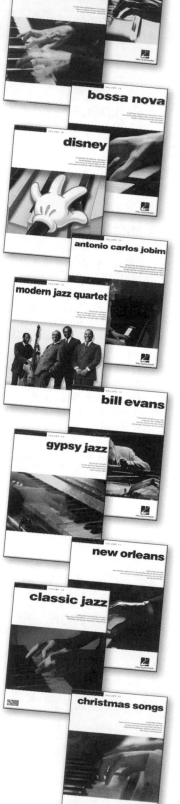

HAL•LEONARD® CORPORATION

7777 W. BLUEMOUND RD. P.O. BOX 13819 MILWAUKEE, WI 53213

www.halleonard.com

Prices, contents and availability subject to change without notice.

0515